Neuro
Autism

Marielle Bayliss

Illustrations by Kellyanne Thorne

GRAFFEG

Hello, I'm Ozzy the neuron.

Come with me on a super-speedy journey through your body!

What is a neuron?

Neurons help with everything your body does. We send messages to your brain. The brain then makes decisions about your movements and feelings.

Need to yawn behind your teacher's back?
Neurons time it to perfection.

Want to win a burping contest? We'll help you belch so loud that it tickles your tonsils!

Woah... that belch was loud! I should know — my job is to send sound signals!

Sound Signals

I live in the inner ear.
I detect and send sound
messages to the brain.

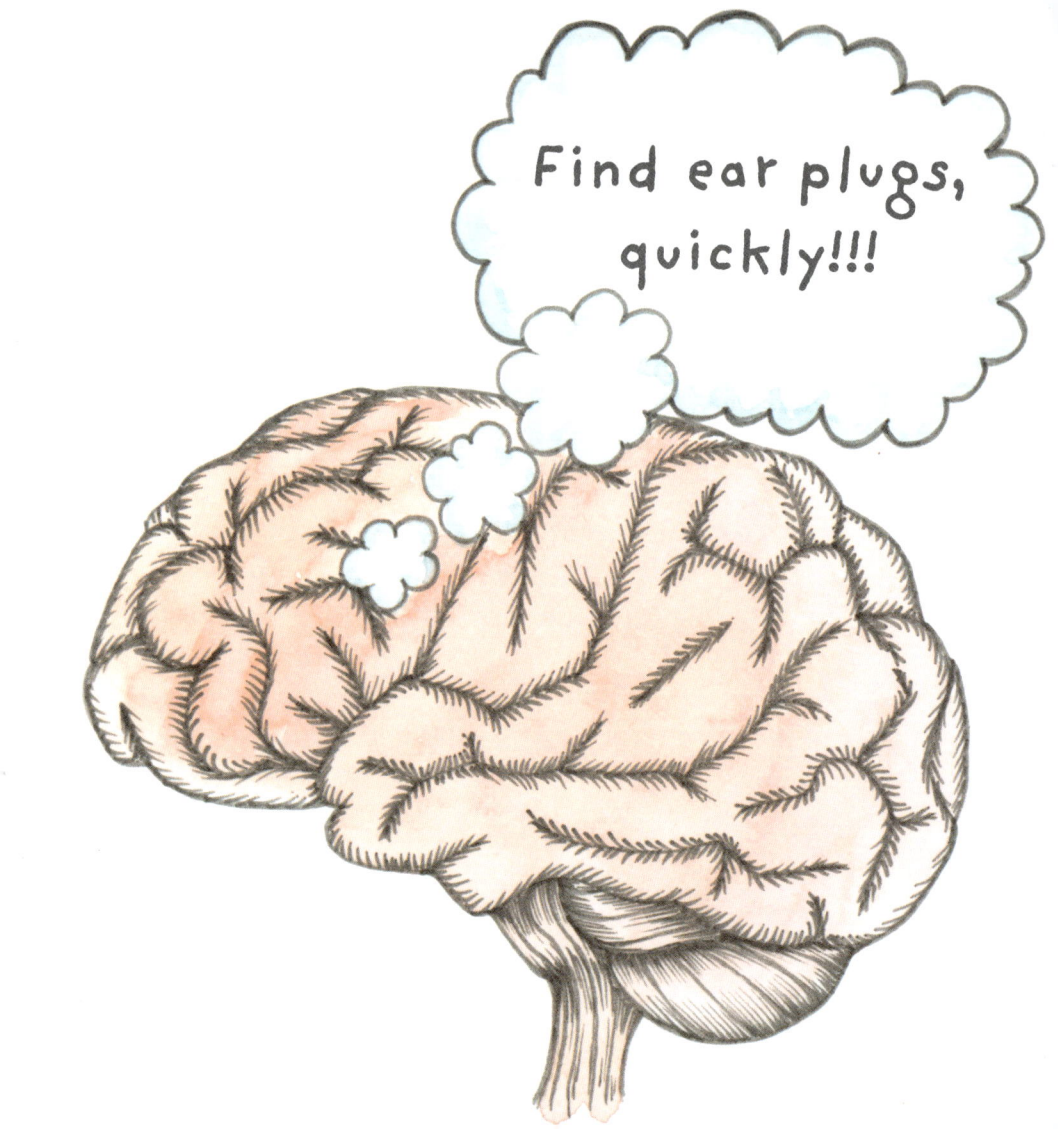

The brain then makes
a decision.

I send complicated sounds...

...or simple noises.

Wait, my neuron senses are tingling...

The lunchtime bell ALWAYS
hurts Amira's ears.

Meet the Spirals

Amira loves music, and so do I!
I play the keyboard and guitar
with my band.
Diva Toonz has a voice
like honey.

Flootz is on flutes!
Beatz is on drums!
Together, we are The Spirals!

When Amira wants to relax, she experiments with new sounds. She loves music, but not the bright stage lights.

She likes being with friends
but doesn't always want to
do the same things.

Sometimes, it feels like others speak in code.

She wishes friends would say what they mean.

New things and people
are tricky...
It's not easy being different.
Amira has autism.

ASC

ASC stands for Autism Spectrum Condition. It's sometimes called a disorder, but Amira doesn't think she has a disorder. Amira likes order. She has excellent focus!

Amira's Autism

Autism can show itself in different ways, that's why we use the term 'spectrum'.

Here are ways that Amira's autism can be tricky:
- It's hard to read people's emotions.
- She doesn't like being hugged.
- Eye contact is difficult.
- She retreats into her own world.
- New things and people are stressful.
- She becomes absorbed in hobbies.
- She's sensitive to loud noises and bright lights.

Sometimes, autism helps Amira:

- She can create her own inner world.
- She expresses thoughts and ideas without fear.
- She's honest and appreciates honesty.
- Is not afraid to ask questions.
- Remembers details.
- Sees things from unique viewpoints.
- She's loyal and doesn't judge others.
- Is passionate about hobbies.

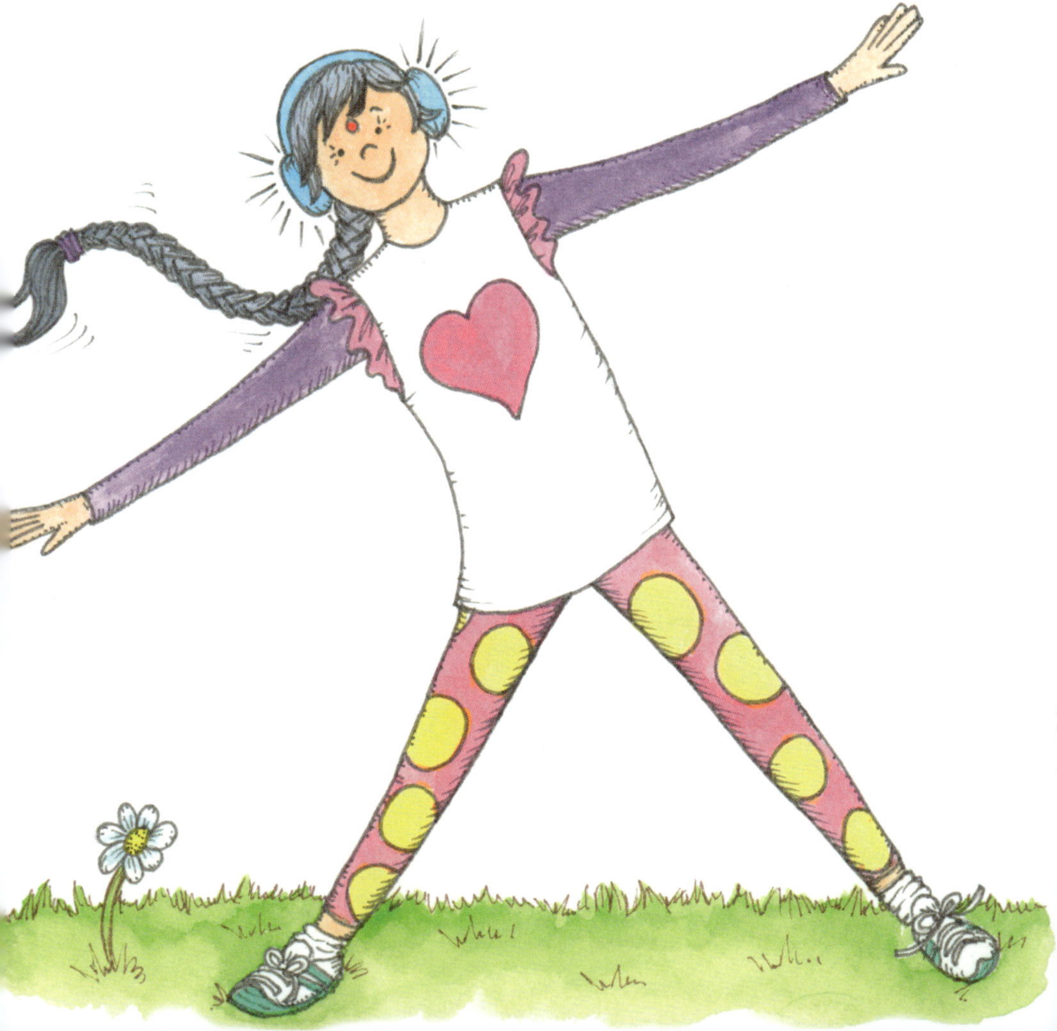

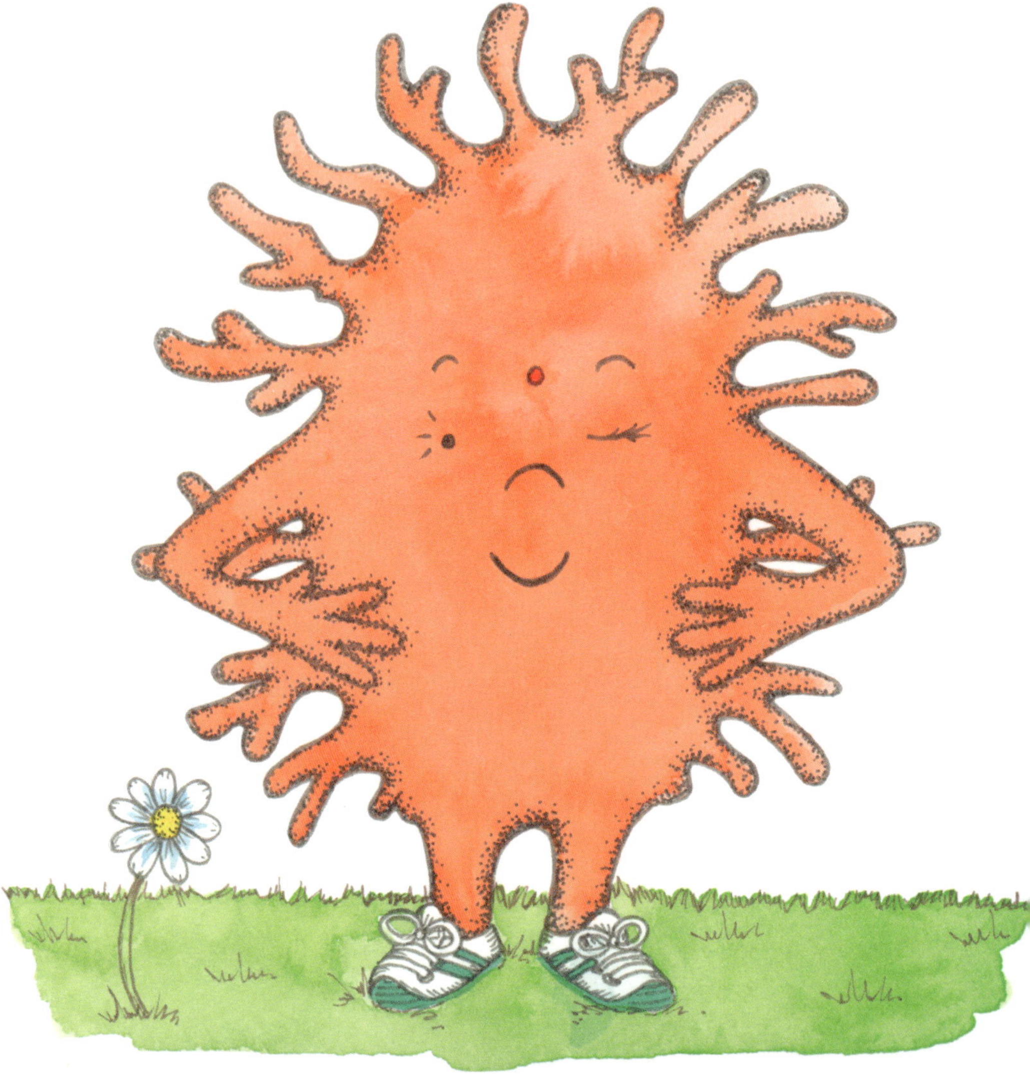

You may notice that some of the things Amira finds tricky can also help her!

Embracing Change

Amira doesn't like new things or change.

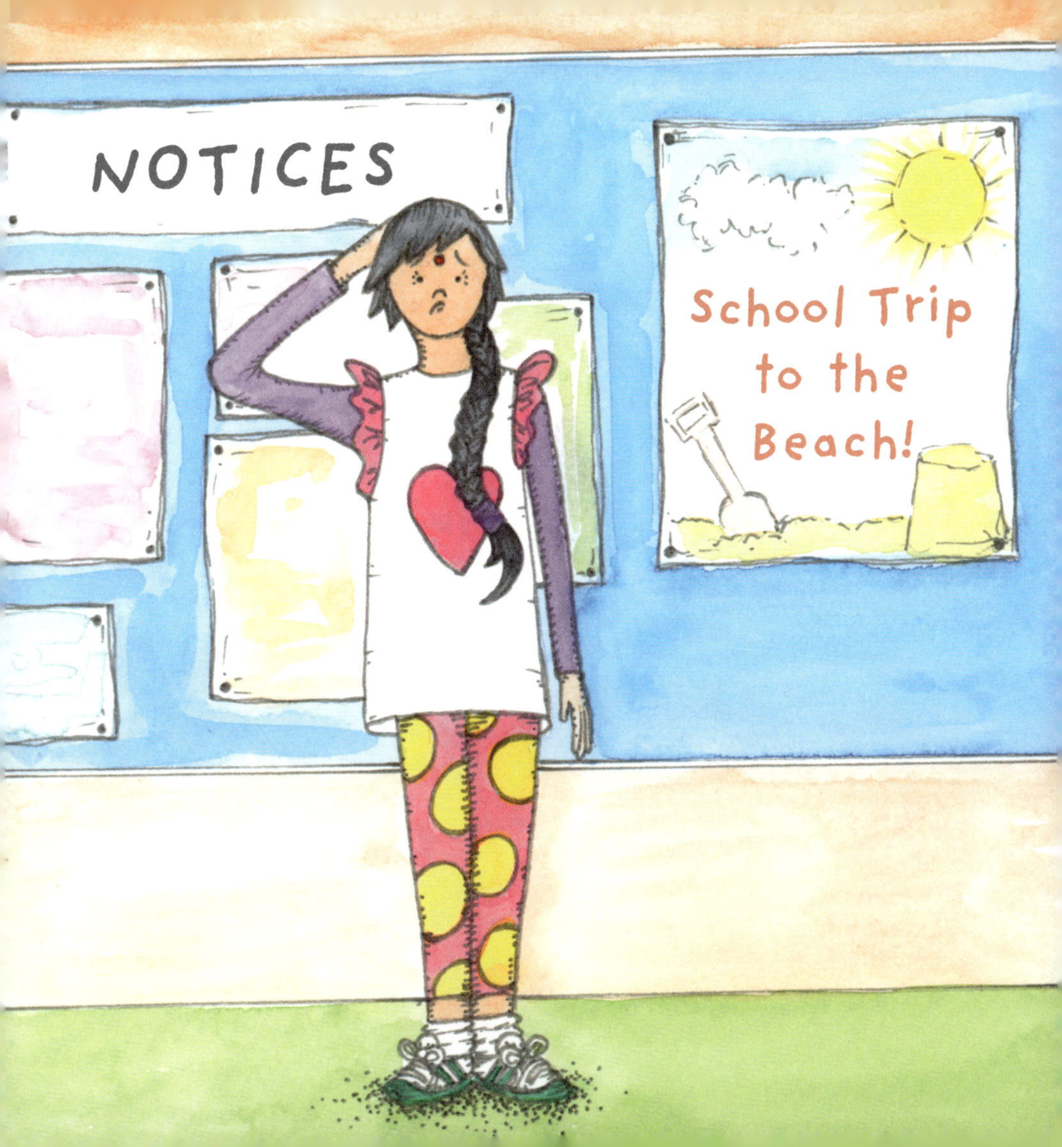
NOTICES
School Trip
to the
Beach!

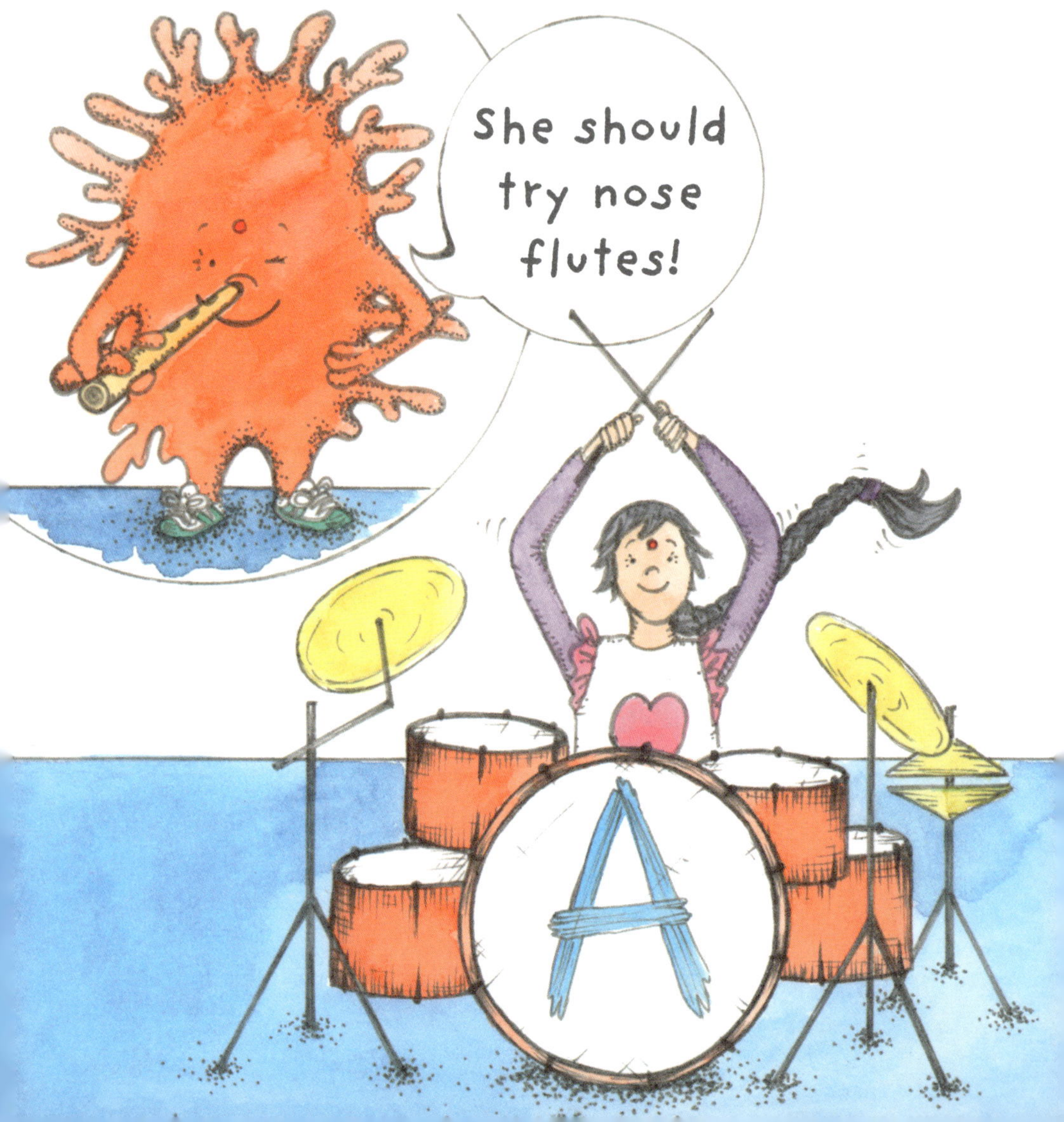
She should try nose flutes!

But in some ways, she's brilliant at adapting to change!

When she's playing music and there's a key change or the timing shifts, Amira changes with it! When she first played drums, it felt wrong, but now she loves it.

Embracing You!

Amira wouldn't change her wonderfully wired brain.

Music is her safe space; it helps her express herself and cope with change. When facing new things, she can bring her safe space with her.

BEACH
THIS WAY

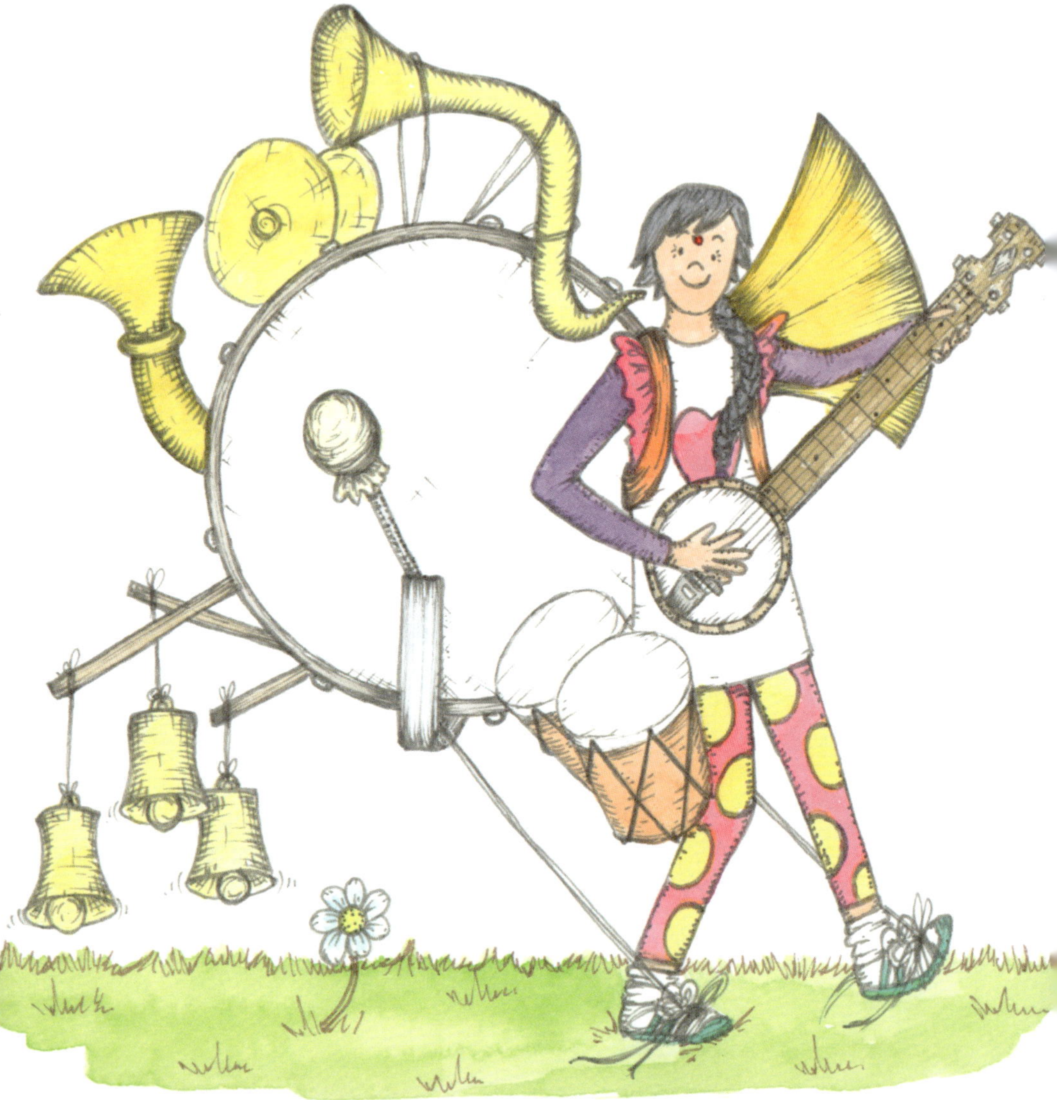

You may have a safe space or hobby that helps. Perhaps you're just starting to find yours?

Change is tricky, but without it there can be no new discoveries!

Neurons and Autism
Published in Great Britain in 2025 by Graffeg Limited.
ISBN 9781802586190

Text copyright © Marielle Bayliss. Illustrations copyright © Kellyanne Thorne. Design and production Graffeg Limited. This publication and content is protected by copyright © 2025.

Graffeg Limited, 15 Neptune Court, Vanguard Way, Cardiff, CF24 5PJ, Wales, UK. Tel: 01554 824000. croeso@graffeg.com. www.graffeg.com

Marielle Bayliss is hereby identified as the author of this work in accordance with section 77 of the Copyright, Designs and Patents Act 1988.

Printed by FINIDR, s.r.o., Czechia.

A CIP Catalogue record for this book is available from the British Library.

All rights reserved. No part of this publication may be reproduced, stored in a retrieval system or transmitted, in any form or by any means, electronic, mechanical, photocopying, recording or otherwise, without the prior permission of the publishers.

This book is designed for children, printed with materials and processes that are safe and meet all applicable European safety requirements. The book does not contain elements that could pose health or safety risks under normal and intended use.

We hereby declare that this product complies with all applicable requirements of the General Product Safety Regulation (GPSR) and any other relevant EU legislation.

Appointed EU Representative:
Easy Access System Europe Oü, 16879218
Mustamäe tee 50, 10621, Tallinn, Estonia
gpsr.requests@easproject.com

The publisher gratefully acknowledges the financial support of this book by the Books Council of Wales. www.gwales.com.

1 2 3 4 5 6 7 8 9

Book Series

Neurons and Epilepsy
ISBN 9781802587821

Neurons and Autism
ISBN 9781802586190

Neurons and Dyspraxia (DCD)
ISBN 9781802587845

Neurons and Dyslexia
ISBN 9781802587852

Neurons and Tourette Syndrome
ISBN 9781802587838

Neurons and ADHD
ISBN 9781802587869

For more information scan the QR code:

Ariennir gan
Lywodraeth Cymru
Funded by
Welsh Government

MIX
Paper from responsible sources
FSC® C014138